WOMEN ON LIFE

A Book of Quotations

Compiled by Rosalie Maggio

This book has also been published under the title
Quotations from Women on Life

MJF BOOKS
NEW YORK

Published by MJF Books
Fine Communications
Two Lincoln Square
60 West 66th Street
New York, NY 10023

Women on Life: A Book of Quotations
LC Control Number 01-130252
ISBN 1-56731-446-5

This edition published by arrangement with Prentice Hall
Direct, a division of Prentice-Hall, Inc.
Excerpts from *The New Beacon Book of Quotations by
Women* (Boston: Beacon Press, 1996) are reprinted with
permission.
This book has also been published under the title
Quotations from Women on Life.

Manufactured in the United States of America on acid-free paper
MJF Books and the MJF colophon are trademarks of
Fine Creative Media, Inc.

10   9   8   7   6   5   4   3   2

Life is like a camel:
you can make it do anything
except back up.

MARCELENE COX

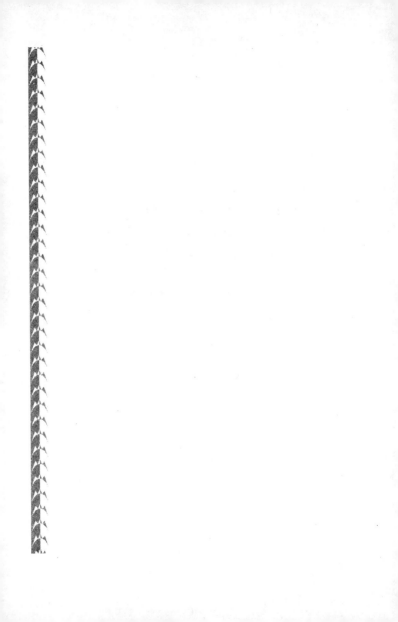

To Liz

$\mathcal{C}$ONTENTS

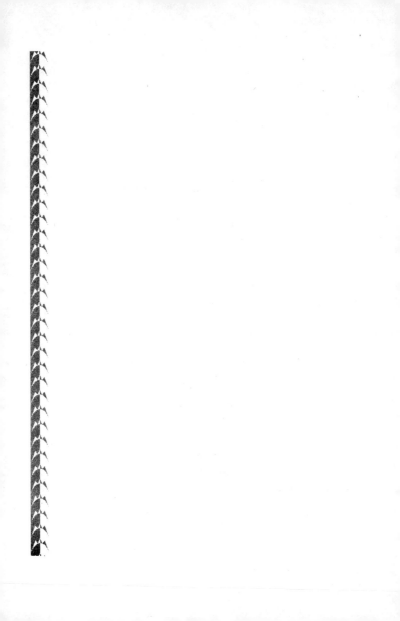

$\mathcal{I}$NTRODUCTION

Life—that wild, unmanageable, and unknowable force both inside us and outside us—can hardly be dealt with adequately in a small book of quotations. But then, the subject of life has not yet been dealt with adequately in all the great learned volumes of philosophy either.

Zora Neale Hurston described folklore as "the boiled-down juice, or pot-likker, of human living." Quotations are also the pot-likker of human living: Other people's ruminations on life, hewed from their questions and doubts and wishful thinking, supply us with that clichéd nutrient, food for thought.

Life seems somehow less shocking, painful, and lonely—and more hopeful, agreeable, and beautiful—when our experiences are confirmed by those of others. Although each of us is unique, there are familiar responses and doubts and joys that let us know we have kin. We are not, after all, too strange to live.

Warped with satisfactions and terrors, woofed with too many ambiguities and too few certainties, life can be lived best not when we have the answers—because we will never have those—but when we know enough to live it right out to the edges, edges sometimes marked by other people, sometimes showing only our own footprints.

There is sexist language in some of the quotations—some women (although not all) followed the arbitrary conventions of earlier times that said the important sex, the default sex, was male. In the other collections of quotations I've compiled I never changed a writer's or speaker's words. However. We all have our weaknesses. I did it for the first time—just once—in this book. Agnes Repplier wrote, "It is in his pleasures that a man really lives, it is from his leisure that he constructs the true fabric of self." This quotation is dear to me; I like to puzzle over just how much truth there is in it. But every time I saw it in the manuscript, I was stopped again by the "his ... man ... his ... he" in a collection about women's lives. I left it. And I left it and I left it. And then I changed it. After her name I've indicated that it's been adapted. What would you have done?

Despite names like Sam Horn, Ralph Iron, Anthony Gilbert, and George Sand, everyone quoted in this book is a woman.

This book is dedicated to a woman with a gift for living life intensely, gracefully, and generously. She is doing the work she was born to do, she is faithful beyond measure to those she loves, and she knows how to find—or create—daily joys in unexpected places and ordinary materials. Should you meet her, you would be charmed by her warmth and enthusiasm and unusual beauty, but what you would always remember would be the sense of having encountered someone who has embraced all that is most wild, unmanageable, and unknowable in life.

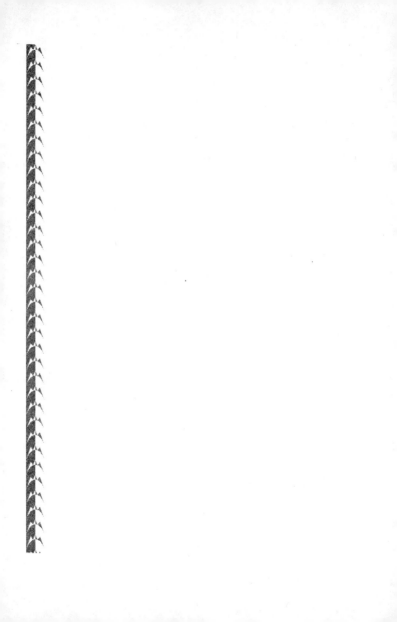

*L*IFE

This is the urgency: Live!
and have your blooming in the noise of the
whirlwind.

GWENDOLYN BROOKS

Warm, eager, living life—to be rooted in life—to
learn, to desire, to know, to feel, to think, to act.
That is what I want. And nothing less. That is what
I must try for.

KATHERINE MANSFIELD

The mere sense of living is joy enough.

EMILY DICKINSON

I like living. I have sometimes been wildly despairing, acutely miserable, racked with sorrow, but through it all I still know quite certainly that just to *be* alive is a grand thing.

AGATHA CHRISTIE

Once out of all the gray days of my life I have looked into the heart of reality; I have witnessed the truth; I have seen life as it really is—ravishingly, ecstatically, madly beautiful, and filled to overflowing with a wild joy, and a value unspeakable.

MARGARET PRESCOTT MONTAGUE

Life is too wonderful,
too full, too short
and strength too limited
to contain its wonder.

RUTH DRAPER

Tell me, what is it you plan to do
with your one wild and precious life?

MARY OLIVER

Don't be afraid your life will end; be afraid that it
will never begin.

GRACE HANSEN

It's not that I'm afraid to die, but I'm terribly,
terribly afraid not to live.

FRANCES NOYES HART

Your life is the one place you have to spend
yourself fully—wild, generous, *drastic*—in an
unrationed profligacy of self. . . . And in that split
second when you understand you finally are
about to die—to uncreate the world no time to do
it over no more chances—that instant when you
realize your conscious existence is truly flaring nova,
won't you want to have used up all—*all*—the
splendor that you are?

ROBIN MORGAN

In masks outrageous and austere
The years go by in single file;
But none has merited my fear,
And none has quite escaped my smile.

ELINOR WYLIE

People living deeply have no fear of death.

ANAÏS NIN

I do not want to arrive at the end of life and then be asked what I made of it and have to answer: "I acted." I want to be able to say: "I loved and I was mystified. It was a joy sometimes, and I knew grief. And I would like to do it all again."

LIV ULLMANN

I don't want to get to the end of my life and find that I lived just the length of it. I want to have lived the width of it as well.

DIANE ACKERMAN

People permit life to slide past them like a deft pick-pocket, their purse—not yet missed and now too late—in his hand.

EDNA FERBER

The day when we plan seriously to start living either never comes or it comes too late.

IDA ALEXA ROSS WYLIE

Perhaps we clutch at life only when we have never lived or trusted it. Then death seems the last and greatest defeat, the end of something never felt.

DOROTHY GILMAN

Am I incapable of living with the one sole guarantee, that I'm still here? Am I afraid of living because I fear death?

HILDEGARD KNEF

It's terrible to realize that you don't learn how to live until you're ready to die; and, then it's too late.

EDNA FERBER

The trouble with many of us is that we just slide along in life. If we would only give, just once, the same amount of reflection to what we want out of life that we give to the question of what to do with a two weeks' vacation, we would be startled at our false standards and the aimless procession of our busy days.

DOROTHY CANFIELD FISHER

Just when summer gets perfect—fresh nights, soft sun, casual breezes, crushingly full and quietly cooling trees, empty beaches, and free weekends—it ends. Life is like that too. Just when we get it right, it starts to change. The job gets easy and we know just how to do it, and they tell us we're retired. The children grow up and get reasonable and they leave home, just when it's nice to have them around. . . . That's life on the edge of autumn. And that's beautiful—if we have the humility for it.

JOAN CHITTISTER

It doesn't matter when life finds you, if it finds you.

KATHLEEN NORRIS

It is never quite safe to think we have done with life. When we imagine we have finished our story fate has a trick of turning the page and showing us yet another chapter.

L.M. MONTGOMERY

You're never too old to become younger.

MAE WEST

How old would you be if you didn't know how old you were?

RUTH GORDON

When one's young . . . everything is a rehearsal. To be repeated ad lib, to be put right when the curtain goes up in earnest. One day you know that the curtain was up all the time. That *was* the performance.

SYBILLE BEDFORD

Funny, isn't it, how your whole life goes by while you think you're only planning the way you're going to live it?

EDNA FERBER

If we get used to life that is the crime.

JEAN GARRIGUE

They are committing murder who merely live.

MAY SARTON

You don't get to choose how you're going to die. Or when. You can only decide how you're going to live. Now.

JOAN BAEZ

The real trick is to stay alive as long as you live.

ANN LANDERS

Life was meant to be lived and curiosity must be kept alive. One must never, for whatever reason, turn one's back on life.

ELEANOR ROOSEVELT

Life seems to love the liver of it.

MAYA ANGELOU

The truth of a life really has little to do with its quality. The quality of life is in proportion, always, to the capacity for delight. The capacity for delight is the gift of paying attention.

JULIA CAMERON

Almost any intense emotion may open our "inward eye" to the beauty of reality. Falling in love appears to do it for some people. The beauties of nature or the exhilaration of artistic creation does it for others. Probably any high experience may momentarily stretch our souls up on tiptoe, so that we catch a glimpse of that marvelous beauty which is always there, but which we are not often tall enough to perceive.

MARGARET PRESCOTT MONTAGUE

Life is the ability to start over again.

JOAN CHITTISTER

Life is a verb, not a noun.

CHARLOTTE PERKINS GILMAN

Life is for most of us a continuous process of getting used to things we hadn't expected.

MARTHA LUPTON

Life itself is the proper binge.

JULIA CHILD

Life need not be easy, provided only that it is not empty.

LISE MEITNER

Life is easier than you'd think; all that is necessary is to accept the impossible, do without the indispensable, and bear the intolerable.

KATHLEEN NORRIS

Life seems to be a choice between two wrong answers.

SHARYN MCCRUMB

The difference is great between one's outside "life," the things which happen to one, incidents, pains and pleasures, and one's "living."

CHARLOTTE PERKINS GILMAN

Are we all living like this? Two lives, the ideal outer life and the inner imaginative life where we keep our secrets?

JEANETTE WINTERSON

Life is a succession of readjustments.

ELIZABETH BOWEN

Life is something that happens to you while you're making other plans.

MARGARET MILLAR

Such a fitful fever life is!

MAY CHRISTIE

Life is a death-defying experience.

EDNA BUCHANAN

Life is a frail moth flying
Caught in the web of the years that pass.

SARA TEASDALE

Life begins when a person first realizes how soon it ends.

MARCELENE COX

It's only when we truly know and understand that we have a limited time on earth—and that we have no way of knowing when our time is up—that we will begin to live each day to the fullest, as if it was the only one we had.

ELISABETH KÜBLER-ROSS

If we had a keen vision and feeling of all ordinary human life, it would be like hearing the grass grow and the squirrel's heart beat, and we should die of the roar which lies on the other side of silence. As it is, the quickest of us walk about well wadded with stupidity.

GEORGE ELIOT

The beauty is forever there before us, forever piping to us, and we are forever failing to dance. We could not help but dance if we could see things as they really are. Then we should kiss both hands to Fate and fling our bodies, hearts, minds, and souls into life with a glorious abandonment, an extravagant, delighted loyalty, knowing that our wildest enthusiasm cannot more than brush the hem of the real beauty and joy and wonder that are always there.

MARGARET PRESCOTT MONTAGUE

I don't want life to imitate art. I want life to *be* art.

CARRIE FISHER

Each day, and the living of it, has to be a conscious creation in which discipline and order are relieved with some play and some pure foolishness.

MAY SARTON

I wanted a perfect ending. Now I've learned the hard way that some poems don't rhyme and some stories don't have a clear beginning, middle and end. Life is about not knowing, having to change, taking the moment and making the best of it, without knowing what is going to happen next. Delicious ambiguity.

GILDA RADNER

Life does not accommodate you, it shatters you. It is meant to, and it couldn't do it better. Every seed destroys its container or else there would be no fruition.

FLORIDA SCOTT-MAXWELL

So few grains of happiness
measured against all the dark
and still the scales balance.

JANE HIRSHFIELD

In spite of the cost of living, it's still popular.

KATHLEEN NORRIS

That's the way the system works. Sometimes you get
the bear, sometimes the bear gets you.

SUE GRAFTON

If logic tells you that life is a meaningless accident,
don't give up on life. Give up on logic.

SHIRA MILGROM

All is waiting and all is work; all is change and all is permanence. All is grace.

BARBARA GRIZZUTI HARRISON

The better life cannot be imposed from without—it must grow from within.

MRS. HUMPHRY WARD

How necessary it is to cultivate a spirit of joy. It is a psychological truth that the physical acts of reverence and devotion make one feel devout. The courteous gesture increases one's respect for others. To act lovingly is to begin to feel loving, and certainly to act joyfully brings joy to others which in turn makes one feel joyful. I believe we are called to the duty of delight.

DOROTHY DAY

I don't believe that life is supposed to make you feel good, or to make you feel miserable either. Life is just supposed to make you feel.

GLORIA NAYLOR

I asked myself the question, "What do you want of your life?" and I realized with a start of recognition and terror, "Exactly what I have—but to be com-mensurate, to handle it all better."

MAY SARTON

We wish for more in life rather than more of it.

JEAN INGELOW

Life is a gamble, a chance, a mere guess. Cast a line
and reel in a splendid rainbow trout or a slippery eel.

MOURNING DOVE

If you take what you want in this world you will also
have to take what you get.

LOUISE REDFIELD PEATTIE

Sacredness of human life! The world has never
believed it! It has been with life that we settled our
quarrels, won wives, gold and land, defended ideas,
imposed religions. We have held that a death toll was
a necessary part of every human achievement,
whether sport, war, or industry. A moment's rage over
the horror of it, and we have sunk into indifference.

IDA TARBELL

If I have learnt anything it is that life forms no logical patterns. It is haphazard and full of beauties which I try to catch as they fly by, for who knows whether any of them will ever return?

MARGOT FONTEYN

It began in mystery, and it will end in mystery, but what a savage and beautiful country lies in between.

DIANE ACKERMAN

I began to have an idea of my life, not as the slow shaping of achievement to fit my preconceived purposes, but as the gradual discovery and growth of a purpose which I did not know.

JOANNA FIELD

It has begun to occur to me that life is a stage I'm going through.

ELLEN GOODMAN

At the moment you are most in awe of all there is about life that you don't understand, you are closer to understanding it all than at any other time.

JANE WAGNER

The mysterious complexity of our life is not to be embraced by maxims . . . to lace ourselves up in formulas of that sort is to repress all the divine promptings and inspirations that spring from growing insight and sympathy.

GEORGE ELIOT

Life is short, and it's up to you to make it sweet.

SADIE DELANY

The hard thing about death is that nothing ever changes. The hard thing about life is that nothing stays the same.

SUE GRAFTON

Life is better than death, I believe, if only because it is less boring, and because it has fresh peaches in it.

ALICE WALKER

Dying is a short horse and soon curried. Living is a horse of another color and bigger.

JESSAMYN WEST

It's not true that life is one damn thing after another—it's one damn thing over and over.

EDNA ST. VINCENT MILLAY

The three horrors of modern life—talk without meaning, desire without love, work without satisfaction.

MIGNON MCLAUGHLIN

It is only after living a fair portion of one's life that one really knows what are the things that matter, the things that will remain unto the end.

ESTHER MEYNELL

The pages of our living turn so silently we scarcely hear them, and it is only afterward that we can look back and say, "That was one chapter."

MARGARET LEE RUNBECK

Life is a thing of many stages and moving parts. What we do with ease at one time of life we can hardly manage at another. What we could not fathom doing when we were young, we find great joy in when we are old. Like the seasons through which we move, life itself is a never-ending series of harvests, a different fruit for every time.

JOAN CHITTISTER

All fruits do not ripen in one season.

LAURE JUNOT

The secret of life is to let every segment of it produce its own yield at its own pace. Every period has something new to teach us. The harvest of youth is achievement; the harvest of middle-age is perspective; the harvest of age is wisdom; the harvest of life is serenity.

JOAN CHITTISTER

Our whole life consists of despairing of an answer and seeking an answer.

DOROTHEE SÖLLE

Time does not dispose of a question — it only presents it anew in a different guise.

AGATHA CHRISTIE

There are years that ask questions and years that answer.

ZORA NEALE HURSTON

Our lives are stories we tell ourselves.

NANCY MAIRS

Never, my heart, is there enough of living.

LÉONIE ADAMS

Why haven't we seventy lives? One is no use.

WINIFRED HOLTBY

Life is like a camel: you can make it do anything except back up.

MARCELENE COX

I learned . . . that one can never go back, that one should not ever try to go back—that the essence of life is going forward. Life is really a one way street, isn't it?

AGATHA CHRISTIE

It seems a silly kind o' business to bring us into the world at all for no special reason 'cept to take us out of it again just as folks 'ave learned to know us a bit and find us useful.

MARIE CORELLI

You live and learn and then you die and forget it all.

LYNNE ALPERN AND ESTHER BLUMENFELD

Life is not so very long.... A little work, a little sleep, a little love, and it is all over.

MARY ROBERTS RINEHART

How short is human life! the very breath!
Which frames my words, accelerates my death.

HANNAH MORE

I took one draft of life —
I'll tell you what I paid —
Precisely an existence —
The market price, they said.

EMILY DICKINSON

If the payment has sometimes been excessive, it was
after all the payment *for life*, and there cannot be
and is no excessive payment for life.

NINA BERBEROVA

When I can look Life in the eyes,
Grown calm and very coldly wise,
Life will have given me the Truth,
And taken in exchange—my youth.

SARA TEASDALE

What you get is a living—what you give is a life.

LILLIAN GISH

That it will never come again
Is what makes life so sweet.

EMILY DICKINSON

Life! Can't live with it, can't live without it.

CYNTHIA NELMS

Life cannot be captured in a few axioms. And that is just what I keep trying to do. But it won't work, for life is full of endless nuances and cannot be captured in just a few formulae.

ETTY HILLESUM

EING

Let's dare to be ourselves, for we do that better than anyone else can.

SHIRLEY BRIGGS

What am I? Nothing. What would I be? Everything.

MARIE BASHKIRTSEFF

What we truly and earnestly aspire *to be*, that in some sense we *are*. The mere aspiration, by changing the frame of the mind, for the moment realizes itself.

ANNA JAMESON

We make ourselves up as we go.

KATE GREEN

Be the most you can be, so life will be more because you were.

SUSAN GLASPELL

Nature never repeats herself, and the possibilities of one human soul will never be found in another.

ELIZABETH CADY STANTON

To want to be what one *can* be is purpose in life.

CYNTHIA OZICK

You need only claim the events of your life to make yourself yours. When you truly possess all you have been and done, which may take some time, you are fierce with reality.

FLORIDA SCOTT-MAXWELL

When I'm trusting and being myself as fully as possible, everything in my life reflects this by falling into place easily, often miraculously.

SHAKTI GAWAIN

If you seek what is honorable, what is good, what is the truth of your life, all the other things you could not imagine come as a matter of course.

OPRAH WINFREY

Anything you do from the heart enriches you, but sometimes not till years later.

MIGNON McLAUGHLIN

I do not want to die . . . until I have faithfully made the most of my talent and cultivated the seed that was placed in me until the last small twig has grown.

KÄTHE KOLLWITZ

I want, by understanding myself, to understand others. I want to be all that I am capable of becoming.

KATHERINE MANSFIELD

Life is a process of *becoming,* a combination of states we have to go through. Where people fail is that they wish to elect a state and remain in it. This is a kind of death.

ANAÏS NIN

We are not born all at once, but by bits. The body first, and the spirit later; and the birth and growth of the spirit, in those who are attentive to their own inner life, are slow and exceedingly painful. Our mothers are racked with the pains of our physical birth; we ourselves suffer the longer pains of our spiritual growth.

MARY ANTIN

A finished person is a boring person.

ANNA QUINDLEN

The gift is that we are unfinished. The sixth day is not yet over for us.

JOANNE GREENBERG

The idea came to me that I *was, am,* and *will be,*
but perhaps will not *become.* This did not scare me.
There was for me in *being* an intensity I did not feel
in *becoming.*

NINA BERBEROVA

A child should be allowed to take as long as she
needs for knowing everything about herself, which is
the same as learning to be herself. Even twenty-five
years if necessary, or even forever. And it wouldn't
matter if doing things got delayed, because nothing
is really important but being oneself.

LAURA RIDING JACKSON

No star is ever lost we once have seen,
We always may be what we might have been.

ADELAIDE ANNE PROCTER

Get rid of the tendency
to judge yourself
above, below, or
equal to others.

ABHIRUPA-NANDA

The world never puts a price on you higher than
the one you put on yourself.

SONJA HENIE

You can be pleased with nothing when you are not
pleased with yourself.

LADY MARY WORTLEY MONTAGU

I didn't learn for years that you generally find your Self after you quit looking for it.

PEG BRACKEN

All my life I've always wanted to *be* somebody. But I see now I should have been more specific.

JANE WAGNER

What you have become is the price you paid to get what you used to want.

MIGNON McLAUGHLIN

Everybody must learn this lesson somewhere—that it costs something to be what you are.

SHIRLEY ABBOTT

No sooner do we think we have assembled a comfortable life than we find a piece of ourselves that has no place to fit in.

GAIL SHEEHY

We are well advised to keep on nodding terms with the people we used to be, whether we find them attractive company or not. Otherwise they run up unannounced and surprise us, come hammering on the mind's door at 4 a.m. of a bad night and demand to know who deserted them, who betrayed them, who is going to make amends.

JOAN DIDION

I'm the kind of woman that likes to enjoy herselves in peace.

ALICE WALKER

It is easier to live through someone else than to become complete yourself.

BETTY FRIEDAN

When, like me, one has nothing in oneself one hopes for everything from another.

COLETTE

I looked always outside of myself to see what I could make the world give me instead of looking within myself to see what was there.

BELLE LIVINGSTONE

I read and walked for miles at night along the beach, writing bad blank verse and searching end-lessly for someone wonderful who would step out of the darkness and change my life. It never crossed my mind that that person could be me.

ANNA QUINDLEN

What a desire! . . . To live in peace with that word: Myself.

SYLVIA ASHTON-WARNER

It matters infinitely less what we *do* than what we *are*.

HARRIET MARTINEAU

We find what we search for—or, if we don't find it, we become it.

JESSAMYN WEST

There are no magics or elves
Or timely godmothers to guide us. We are lost, must
Wizard a track through our own screaming weed.

GWENDOLYN BROOKS

Beingness, doingness and havingness are like a
triangle where each side supports the others. They
are not in conflict with each other. They all exist
simultaneously. Often people attempt to live their
lives backwards: They try to *have* more things, or
more money, in order to *do* more of what they want,
so that they will *be* happier. The way it actually
works is the reverse. You must first *be* who you really
are, then *do* what you need to do, in order to *have*
what you want.

SHAKTI GAWAIN

DOING

What you will do matters. All you need is to do it.

JUDY GRAHN

I don't waste time thinking, "Am I doing it right?" I say, "Am I doing it?"

GEORGETTE MOSBACHER

It will never rain roses: when we want
To have more roses we must plant more trees.

GEORGE ELIOT

Everything we do seeds the future. No action is an empty one.

JOAN CHITTISTER

If it is to be, it is up to me.

SHIRLEY HUTTON

It is better to wear out than to rust out.

FRANCES E. WILLARD

One's only real regret in life is the failure to act.

JANE STANTON HITCHCOCK

Inaction, contrary to its reputation for being a refuge, is neither safe nor comfortable.

MADELEINE KUNIN

The thing that destroys a person/a people
is not the knowing
but the knowing and not
doing.

CAROLYN M. RODGERS

What you don't do can be a destructive force.

ELEANOR ROOSEVELT

The most ominous of fallacies—the belief that
things can be kept static by inaction.

FREYA STARK

Perhaps it is impossible for a person who does no
good not to do harm.

HARRIET BEECHER STOWE

So much attention is paid to the aggressive sins, such as violence and cruelty and greed with all their tragic effects, that too little attention is paid to the passive sins, such as apathy and laziness, which in the long run can have a more devastating and destructive effect upon society than the others.

ELEANOR ROOSEVELT

There are so many things that we wish we had done yesterday, so few that we feel like doing today.

MIGNON MCLAUGHLIN

Every year I live I am more convinced that the waste of life lies in the love we have not given, the powers we have not used, the selfish prudence that will risk nothing . . . . No one ever yet was the poorer in the long run for having once in a lifetime "let out all the length of the reins."

MARY CHOLMONDELEY

It isn't the thing you do, Dear
It's the thing you leave undone
Which gives you a bit of a heartache
At the setting of the sun.

MARGARET E. SANGSTER

We might have been!—these are but common words,
And yet they make the sum of life's bewailing.

L.E. LANDON

The bitterest tears shed over graves are for words left
unsaid and deeds left undone.

CHRISTOPHER CROWFIELD

I have made it a rule of my life never to regret and never to look back. Regret is an appalling waste of energy. . . . You can't build on it; it's only good for wallowing in.

KATHERINE MANSFIELD

What does so-called success or failure matter if only you have succeeded in doing the thing you set out to do. The *doing* is all that really counts.

EVA LE GALLIENNE

The ideal life is to do everything a little and one thing a lot.

MARTHA LUPTON

There can be no happiness if the things we believe in are different from the things we do.

FREYA STARK

I think knowing what you can *not* do is more important than knowing what you can do.

LUCILLE BALL

Most people are so busy knocking themselves out trying to do everything they think they should do, they never get around to what they want to do.

KATHLEEN WINSOR

The things that one most wants to do are the things that are probably most worth doing.

WINIFRED HOLTBY

It takes time and trouble to persuade ourselves that the things we want to do are the things we ought to do.

AGNES REPPLIER

What you wish to do you are apt to think you ought to do.

MARIE VON EBNER-ESCHENBACH

"Ought"! What an ugly word *that* is!

PHYLLIS BOTTOME

Do what you want to do, when you want to do it . . . and not a moment sooner.

OPRAH WINFREY

Life engenders life. Energy creates energy. It is by spending oneself that one becomes rich.

SARAH BERNHARDT

*H*AVING

You can have anything you want if you want it desperately enough. You must want it with an inner exuberance that erupts through the skin and joins the energy that created the world.

SHEILAH GRAHAM

It is inevitable that when one has a great need of something one finds it. What you need you attract like a lover.

GERTRUDE STEIN

One gets . . . not what one wants but what one is.

DODIE SMITH

Perhaps all human progress stems from the tension between two basic drives: to have just what everyone else has and to have what no one has.

JUDITH STONE

Nothing makes you realize you don't know what you want more than getting what you want.

JANE WAGNER

I never wanted what I thought I wanted
But always something else
Which changed again as soon as I had found it.

MARY CAROLYN DAVIES

We are all more blind to what we have than to what we have not.

AUDRE LORDE

Until you make peace with who you are, you'll never be content with what you have.

DORIS MORTMAN

You already possess all you need to be genuinely happy.

SARAH BAN BREATHNACH

It's possible to have too much in life. Too many clothes jade our appreciation for new ones; too much money can put us out of touch with life; too much free time can dull the edge of the soul. We need sometimes to come very near the bone so that we can taste the marrow of life rather than its superfluities.

JOAN CHITTISTER

Frugality is one of the most beautiful and joyful words in the English language, and yet it is one that we are culturally cut off from understanding and enjoying. The consumption society has made us feel that happiness lies in having things, and has failed to teach us the happiness of not having things.

ELISE BOULDING

I have the greatest of all riches: that of not desiring them.

ELEANORA DUSE

Simplicity is the most difficult thing to secure in this world; it is the last limit of experience and the last effort of genius.

GEORGE SAND

We go on multiplying our conveniences only to multiply our cares. We increase our possessions only to the enlargement of our anxieties.

ANNA C. BRACKETT

If my hands are fully occupied in holding on to something, I can neither give nor receive.

DOROTHEE SÖLLE

A cup that is already full cannot have more added to it. In order to receive the further good to which we are entitled, we must give of that which we have.

MARGARET BECKER

I suppose you can't have everything, though my instinctive response to this sentiment is always, "Why not?"

MARGARET HALSEY

HAPPINESS

Each moment in time we have it all, even when we think we don't.

MELODY BEATTIE

Happiness is nothing but everyday living seen through a veil.

ZORA NEALE HURSTON

Happiness consists not in having much, but in being content with little.

COUNTESS OF BLESSINGTON

We are all given the ingredients of happiness, but the mixing is left to ourselves.

Ethel M. Dell

Getting what you go after is success; but liking it while you are getting it is happiness.

Bertha Damon

Happiness lies in the consciousness we have of it.

George Sand

We are ourselves the stumbling-blocks in the way of our happiness. Place a common individual—by common, I mean with the common share of stupidity, custom, and discontent—place him in the garden of Eden, and he would not find it out unless he were told, and when told, he would not believe it.

L.E. Landon

The greater part of our happiness or misery depends on our dispositions, and not on our circumstances. We carry the seeds of the one or the other about with us in our minds wherever we go.

MARTHA WASHINGTON

Happiness is a work of art. Handle with care.

EDITH WHARTON

What we do modifies us more than what is done to us.

CHARLOTTE PERKINS GILMAN

The world seems to be divided into two groups of people: those who say you can never get something for nothing, and those muddled but happy creatures who maintain that the best things in life are free.

JANET GILLESPIE

I make the most of all that comes,
The least of all that goes.

SARA TEASDALE

The genius for happiness is still so rare, is indeed on the whole the rarest genius. To possess it means to approach life with the humility of a beggar, but to treat it with the proud generosity of a prince; to bring to its totality the deep understanding of a great poet and to each of its moments the abandonment and ingenuousness of a child.

ELLEN KEY

I hold those wise who know how to be happy.

NINON DE LENCLOS

It is not easy to find happiness in ourselves, and it is not possible to find it elsewhere.

AGNES REPPLIER

Happiness comes of the capacity to feel deeply, to enjoy simply, to think freely, to risk life, to be needed.

STORM JAMESON

Those persons are happiest in this restless and mutable world who are in love with change, who delight in what is new simply because it differs from what is old; who rejoice in every innovation, and find a strange alert pleasure in all that is, and that has never been before.

AGNES REPPLIER

O world, I cannot hold thee close enough!

EDNA ST. VINCENT MILLAY

Surely the strange beauty of the world must somewhere rest on pure joy!

LOUISE BOGAN

There is no such thing as the pursuit of happiness, but there is the discovery of joy.

JOYCE GRENFELL

The joy of a spirit is the measure of its power.

NINON DE LENCLOS

There is a curriculum in living in which I have not studied. This may be happiness. I want to know it; I should feel better prepared for immortality. I do not wish to arrive fagged at last and a bit slipshod in the spirit, as if I had a hard time all my mortal life. It is not complimentary to God.

CORRA HARRIS

Think of all the beauty that's still left in and around you and be happy!

ANNE FRANK

Abundance is, in large part, an attitude.

SUE PATTON THOELE

The more you praise and celebrate your life, the more there is in life to celebrate. The more you complain, the more you find fault, the more misery and fault you will have to find.

OPRAH WINFREY

Gratitude unlocks the fullness of life. It turns what we have into enough, and more. It turns denial into acceptance, chaos to order, confusion to clarity. It can turn a meal into a feast, a house into a home, a stranger into a friend. Gratitude makes sense of our past, brings peace for today, and creates a vision for tomorrow.

MELODY BEATTIE

There's a self-expansive aspect of gratitude. Very possibly it's a little-known law of nature: the more gratitude you have, the more you have to be grateful for.

ELAINE ST. JAMES

Once we learn to count our blessings they increase.

STELLA TERRILL MANN

Blessed are those who can give without remembering, and take without forgetting.

ELIZABETH BIBESCO

To view your life as blessed does not require you to deny your pain. It simply demands a more complicated vision, one in which a condition or event is not either good or bad but is, rather, both good and bad, not sequentially but simultaneously.

NANCY MAIRS

Where there is laughter there is always more health than sickness.

PHYLLIS BOTTOME

If you can laugh at it, you can live with it.

ERMA BOMBECK

A good laugh is as good as a prayer sometimes.

L.M. MONTGOMERY

Total absence of humor renders life impossible.

COLETTE

The bad things of life were very transitory. It was the good things, the ribbed sand, the wind blowing over the white-capped waves, the sunshine and the stars, that were so tough and durable.

ELIZABETH GOUDGE

The bad times I can handle. It's the good times that drive me crazy. When is the other shoe going to drop?

ERMA BOMBECK

A successful life for a man or for a woman seems to me to lie in the knowledge that one has developed to the limit the capacities with which one was endowed; that one has contributed something constructive to family and friends and to a home community; that one has brought happiness wherever it was possible; that one has earned one's way in the world, has kept some friends, and need not be ashamed to face oneself honestly.

ELEANOR ROOSEVELT

Know the difference between success and fame. Success is Mother Teresa. Fame is Madonna.

ERMA BOMBECK

*T*URNING POINTS

When you can't see straight ahead, it's because you're about to turn a corner.

MYRTLE REED

The strongest principle of growth lies in human choice.

GEORGE ELIOT

Choice is the essence of what I believe it is to be human.

LIV ULLMANN

It is the ability to choose which makes us human.

MADELEINE L'ENGLE

It's when we're given choice that we sit with the gods and design ourselves.

DOROTHY GILMAN

A peacefulness follows any decision, even the wrong one.

RITA MAE BROWN

What is living about? It is the decisions you must make between two rights, hard and costly decisions because always you can do one right thing, but sometimes not two.

WILLA GIBBS

No trumpets sound when the important decisions of our life are made. Destiny is made known silently.

AGNES DE MILLE

Only in growth, reform, and change, paradoxically enough, is true security to be found.

ANNE MORROW LINDBERGH

Change is the constant, the signal for rebirth, the egg of the phoenix.

CHRISTINA BALDWIN

Life is change: growth is optional.

KAREN KAISER CLARK

You make what seems a simple choice: choose a man or a job or a neighborhood—and what you have chosen is not a man or a job or a neighborhood, but a life.

JESSAMYN WEST

Autumn to winter, winter into spring,
Spring into summer, summer into fall—
So rolls the changing year, and so we change;
Motion so swift, we know not that we move.

DINAH MARIA MULOCK CRAIK

The change of life is the time when you meet yourself at a crossroads and you decide whether to be honest or not before you die.

KATHARINE BUTLER HATHAWAY

When you're stuck in a spiral, to change all aspects of the spin you need only to change one thing.

CHRISTINA BALDWIN

There is always new life trying to emerge in each of us. Too often we ignore the signs of resurrection and cling to parts of life that have died for us.

JOAN CHITTISTER

Neither situations nor people can be altered by the interference of an outsider. If they are to be altered, that alteration must come from within.

PHYLLIS BOTTOME

Nourish beginnings, let us nourish beginnings.
Not all things are blest, but the
seeds of all things are blest.
The blessing is in the seed.

MURIEL RUKEYSER

No first step can be really great; it must of necessity possess more of prophecy than of achievement; nevertheless it is by the first step that a man marks the value, not only of his cause, but of himself.

KATHERINE CECIL THURSTON

All birth is unwilling.

PEARL S. BUCK

The world is round and the place which may seem like the end may also be only the beginning.

IVY BAKER PRIEST

It isn't the things that happen to us, it's the things we think are going to happen to us that drive us almost crazy.

KATHLEEN NORRIS

If we can recognize that change and uncertainty are basic principles, we can greet the future and the transformation we are undergoing with the understanding that *we do not know enough to be pessimistic.*

HAZEL HENDERSON

Life is so constructed, that the event does not, cannot, will not, match the expectation.

CHARLOTTE BRONTË

Living is a form of not being sure, not knowing what's next or how.

AGNES DE MILLE

Things come suitable to the time.

ENID BAGNOLD

Some things . . . arrive in their own mysterious hour, on their own terms and not yours, to be seized or relinquished forever.

GAIL GODWIN

Truly nothing is to be expected but the unexpected!

ALICE JAMES

If you do nothing unexpected, nothing unexpected happens.

FAY WELDON

The only thing that makes life possible is permanent, intolerable uncertainty: not knowing what comes next.

URSULA K. LEGUIN

I am not wise. Not knowing, and learning to be comfortable with not knowing, is a great discovery.

SUE BENDER

Only people who die very young learn all they really need to know in kindergarten.

WENDY KAMINER

When you get in a tight place and everything goes against you till it seems as though you could not hold on a minute longer, never give up then, for that is just the time and the place the tide will turn.

HARRIET BEECHER STOWE

I try to tell people to keep having hope. It's always what you don't know and don't expect that's gonna be so great.

ROSEANNE BARR

PASSION

We must have a passion in life.

GEORGE SAND

It is the soul's duty to be loyal to its own desires. It must abandon itself to its master passion.

REBECCA WEST

I believe we come to earth with sealed orders. I believe that only those who lack passion look down on purpose.

LIV ULLMANN

The fiery moments of passionate experience are the moments of wholeness and totality of the personality.

ANAÏS NIN

When it's over, I want to say: all my life
I was a bride married to amazement.
I was the bridegroom, taking the world into my arms.

MARY OLIVER

Enthusiasm is contagious. Be a carrier.

SUSAN RABIN

The one who cares the most wins. . . . That's how I
knew I'd end up with everyone else waving the
white flags and not me. That's how I knew I'd be the
last person standing when it was all over. . . . I cared
the most.

ROSEANNE BARR

A short life in the saddle, Lord!
Not long life by the fire.

LOUISE IMOGEN GUINEY

People do not live nowadays—they get about ten percent out of life.

ISADORA DUNCAN

Better to be without logic than without feeling.

CHARLOTTE BRONTË

I am one of those people who just can't help getting a kick out of life—even when it's a kick in the teeth.

POLLY ADLER

When you consider something like death, after which (there being no news flash to the contrary) we may well go out like a candle flame, then it probably doesn't matter if we try too hard, are awkward sometimes, care for one another too deeply, are excessively curious about nature, are too open to experience, enjoy a nonstop expense of the senses in an effort to know life intimately and lovingly.

DIANE ACKERMAN

It is impossible to drive out human passions from the human heart. You may suppress them, deaden them, keep them in subjection, but you cannot root them out.

MRS. HENRY WOOD

She would not rest until existence was for her a sucked orange. When there was no drop of juice left, then she would fling away the rind and die content.

ELIZABETH GOUDGE

ISK

Life is either a daring adventure or nothing. To keep our faces toward change and behave like free spirits in the presence of fate is strength undefeatable.

HELEN KELLER

The only difference between a rut and a grave . . . is in their dimensions.

ELLEN GLASGOW

Sometimes I wonder what the difference is between being cautious and being dead.

SUE GRAFTON

All adventuring is rash, and all innovations dangerous. But not nearly so dangerous as stagnation and
dry rot. From grooves, cliques, clichés and resigna-
tion—Good Lord deliver us!

WINIFRED HOLTBY

The fullness of life is in the hazards of life.

EDITH HAMILTON

If you risk nothing, then you risk everything.

GEENA DAVIS

If you don't risk anything, you risk even *more*.

ERICA JONG

Playing it safe is the riskiest choice we can ever make.

SARAH BAN BREATHNACH

To be tested is good. The challenged life may be the best therapist.

GAIL SHEEHY

Thank goodness for people courageous enough to be ridiculous, if they must be, in order to balance their lives.

KATHARINE BUTLER HATHAWAY

If you're never scared or embarrassed or hurt, it means you never take any chances.

JULIA SOREL

Life shrinks or expands in proportion to one's courage.

ANAÏS NIN

The only courage that matters is the kind that gets you from one moment to the next.

MIGNON MCLAUGHLIN

You must do the thing you think you cannot do.

ELEANOR ROOSEVELT

When people keep telling you that you can't do a thing, you kind of like to try it.

MARGARET CHASE SMITH

Hard Times

It is easy enough to be pleasant
When life flows by like a song,
But the man worth while is the one who will smile
When everything goes dead wrong.

ELLA WHEELER WILCOX

Sometimes it feels like God has reached down and touched me, blessed me a thousand times over, and sometimes it all feels like a mean joke, like God's advisers are Muammar Qaddafi and Phyllis Schlafly.

ANNE LAMOTT

It's always something.

GILDA RADNER

No matter how one's heart aches, one can do the necessary things and do them well.

MYRTLE REED

Birds sing after a storm; why shouldn't people feel as free to delight in whatever sunlight remains to them?

ROSE KENNEDY

Flowers grow
out of the dark
moments.

CORITA KENT

A depressing and difficult passage has prefaced every new page I have turned in life.

CHARLOTTE BRONTË

Surviving and believing in tomorrow is just a habit I can't break.

MARITA GOLDEN

Build for yourself a strongbox,
Fashion each part with care;
When it's strong as your hand can make it,
Put all your troubles there . . .
Lock all your heartaches within it,
Then sit on the lid and laugh.

BERTHA ADAMS BACKUS

You must learn to drink the cup of life as it comes . . . without stirring it up from the bottom. That's where the bitter dregs are.

AGNES TURNBULL

The great crises of life are not, I think, necessarily those which are in themselves the hardest to bear, but those for which we are least prepared.

MARY ADAMS

Every life has a death, and every light a shadow. Be content to stand in the light, and let the shadow fall where it will.

MARY STEWART

Keep your face to the sunshine and you cannot see the shadow.

HELEN KELLER

When we were children, we used to think that when we were grown-up we would no longer be vulnerable. But to grow up is to accept vulnerability. . . . To be alive is to be vulnerable.

MADELEINE L'ENGLE

As wise women and men in every culture tell us:
The art of life is not controlling what happens to us,
but *using* what happens to us.

GLORIA STEINEM

There is hardly a problem, no matter how complicated it is, that when looked at in the right way does-
n't become still more complicated.

PEG BRACKEN

This alone is to be feared—the closed mind, the
sleeping imagination, the death of the spirit. The
death of the body is to that, I think, a little thing.

WINIFRED HOLTBY

Life is not always what one wants it to be, but to make the best of it as it is, is the only way of being happy.

JENNIE JEROME CHURCHILL

I once considered writing a book called *I'm Not OK and You're Not OK, and That's OK.*

ELISABETH KÜBLER-ROSS

The same fire that hardens the egg will melt the butter; and much depends on the personality type, whether you customarily rise to a challenge or whether you sink. For as long as I can remember, I have been a sinker. One challenge, and I drop like a rock.

PEG BRACKEN

If you can't make a mistake, you can't make anything.

MARVA COLLINS

Just because you *made* a mistake doesn't mean you *are* a mistake.

GEORGETTE MOSBACHER

To weep over a folly is to double it.

MINNA THOMAS ANTRIM

The habit of shutting doors behind us is invaluable to happiness; we must learn to shut life's doors to cut out the futile wind of past mistakes.

MARJORIE HOLMES

In retrospect, our triumphs could as easily have happened to someone else; but our defeats are uniquely our own.

MIGNON MCLAUGHLIN

When we yield to discouragement it is usually because we give too much thought to the past and to the future.

ST. THÉRÈSE OF LISIEUX

Learning too soon our limitations, we never learn our powers.

MIGNON MCLAUGHLIN

No matter how old we get, life's always got a lesson for you. Most likely one you've learned ten times before.

BARBARA NEELY

There's always room for improvement—it's the biggest room in the house.

LOUISE HEATH LEBER

Mistakes are doorways to discovery.

SAM HORN

Because we are always staring at the stars, we learn the shortness of our arms.

MARY ROBERTS RINEHART

It's easy to get a reputation for wisdom. It's only necessary to live long, speak little and do less.

P.D. JAMES

The unwillingness to try
is worse than any failure.

NIKKI GIOVANNI

For yesterday and for all tomorrows, we dance the best we know.

KATE SEREDY

By our errors we see deeper into life.

RALPH IRON

There is always a time to make right what is wrong.

SUSAN GRIFFIN

Men don't make different mistakes at different periods of their lives. They make the same mistake over and over again and they pay a bigger and bigger price for it.

VICKI BAUM

It isn't true, by the way, that nothing is as bad as you think it's going to be. Some things are exactly as bad as you thought they were going to be, and some things are worse.

PEG BRACKEN

Mine was a life of failure—one thing after another—like most lives . . . but that is all right, it is universal, it is the great human experience to fail.

KATHARINE BUTLER HATHAWAY

I've never found anything whatsoever that is as easy to do the right way as the wrong way, and if there is such a thing I would like to know about it.

PEG BRACKEN

Mistakes are a fact of life
It is the response to error that counts.

NIKKI GIOVANNI

Failure?
I'm not ashamed to tell it,
I never learned to spell it.
Not Failure.

MAYA ANGELOU

Failure is just another way to learn how to do something right.

MARIAN WRIGHT EDELMAN

A series of failures may culminate in the best possible result.

GISELA M.A. RICHTER

Sometimes what you want to do *has* to fail so you won't.

MARGUERITTE HARMON BRO

People fail forward to success.

MARY KAY ASH

Some of the biggest failures I ever had were successes.

PEARL BAILEY

Apparent failure may hold in its rough shell the germs of a success that will blossom in time, and bear fruit throughout eternity.

FRANCES ELLEN WATKINS HARPER

No honest work of man or woman "fails";
It feeds the sum of all human action.

MICHELENE WANDOR

If you have made mistakes, even serious ones, there is always another chance for you. What we call failure is not the falling down, but the staying down.

MARY PICKFORD

The sheer rebelliousness in giving ourselves permission to fail frees a childlike awareness and clarity . . . . When we give ourselves permission to fail, we at the same time give ourselves permission to excel.

ELOISE RISTAD

Success and failure are both greatly overrated but failure gives you a whole lot more to talk about.

HILDEGARD KNEF

When you get to the end of your rope—tie a knot in it and hang on.

ELEANOR ROOSEVELT

I will tell you that there have been no failures in my life. I don't want to sound like some metaphysical queen, but there have been no failures. There have been some tremendous lessons.

OPRAH WINFREY

We may encounter many defeats but we must not be defeated.

MAYA ANGELOU

There is hope for all of us. Well, anyway, if you don't die you live through it, day in, day out.

MARY BECKETT

All that is necessary to break the spell of inertia and frustration is this: *Act as if it were impossible to fail.* That is the talisman, the formula, the command of right-about-face which turns us from failure towards success.

DOROTHEA BRANDE

The worst of my life is over,
I hope,
And may the best things, please,
come soon.

CORAZON C. AQUINO

USYNESS

Time is always wanting to me, and I cannot meet
with a single day when I am not hurried along,
driven to my wits'-end by urgent work, business to
attend to, or some service to render.

GEORGE SAND

Too many people, too many demands, too much to
do; competent, busy, hurrying people—It just isn't
living at all.

ANNE MORROW LINDBERGH

We are always doing something, talking, reading,
listening to the radio, planning what next. The mind
is kept naggingly busy on some easy, unimportant
external thing all day.

BRENDA UELAND

People who are genuinely involved in life, not just living a routine they've contrived to protect them from disaster, always seem to have more demanded of them than they can easily take on.

AMANDA CROSS

Life is walking fast
It wasn't how I wanted it, but I had to take what I could.

VÉRONIQUE TADJO

Her life was like running on a treadmill or riding on a stationary bike; it was aerobic, it was healthy, but she wasn't going anywhere.

JULIA PHILLIPS

The speed of life on the fast track permeates every area of our lives. Hurrying becomes a *habit*.

ELAINE ST. JAMES

With the only certainty in our daily existence being change, and a rate of change growing always faster in a kind of technological leapfrog game, speed helps people think they are keeping up.

GAIL SHEEHY

Not all speed is movement.

TONI CADE

All change is not growth; all movement is not forward.

ELLEN GLASGOW

I'd been busy, busy, so busy, preparing for life, while life floated by me, quiet and swift as a regatta.

LORENE CARY

My days ran away so fast. I simply ran after my days.

LEAH MORTON

Oh bolting Time, rough pony of my days,
Halt by the hedgerow of my life to graze.

VITA SACKVILLE-WEST

Women aren't trying to do too much. Women *have*
too much to do.

MARY KAY BLAKELY

We need time to dream, time to remember, and
time to reach the infinite. Time to be.

GLADYS TABER

One could do with a longer year—so much to do, so little done, alas.

ROSE MACAULAY

We miss a lot in life because we don't know when to quit, what to leave out.

ETHEL WATERS

Living fully doesn't mean having it all, going everywhere, doing everything, and being all things to all people. Many of us are beginning to see that too much *is* too much.

ELAINE ST. JAMES

Life comes in clusters, clusters of solitude, then a cluster when there is hardly time to breathe.

MAY SARTON

Oh, time betrays us. Time is the great enemy.

WINIFRED HOLTBY

People used to have time to live and enjoy themselves, but there is no time anymore for anything
but work, work, work.

LAURA INGALLS WILDER

Why is life speeded up so? Why are things so terribly, unbearably precious that you can't enjoy them
but can only wait breathless in dread of their going?

ANNE MORROW LINDBERGH

There is too much doing—too little being! When we
begin to get strenuous, life begins to grow intolerable.

MARTHA OSTENSO

What we lack is not so much leisure to *do* as time to reflect and time to feel. What we seldom "take" is time to experience the things that have happened, the things that are happening, the things that are still ahead of us.

MARGARET MEAD AND RHODA METRAUX

It is in our pleasure that we really live; it is from our leisure that we construct the true fabric of self.

AGNES REPPLIER (ADAPTED)

I recently adopted for my own a good motto I saw somewhere, on a barroom mirror or possibly a washroom wall: "The time you enjoyed wasting wasn't wasted." I think I'll have that printed some day on a T-shirt or the bedroom ceiling.

PEG BRACKEN

The ultimate of being successful is the luxury of giving yourself the time to do what you want to do.

LEONTYNE PRICE

It is in our idleness, in our dreams, that the submerged truth sometimes comes to the top.

VIRGINIA WOOLF

I've dreamt in my life dreams that have stayed with me ever after, and changed my ideas: they've gone through and through me, like wine through water, and altered the color of my mind.

EMILY BRONTË

Dreams are . . . an expansion of life, an enlightenment, and a discipline. I thank God for my dream life; my daily life would be far poorer, if it wanted the second sight of dreams.

AMELIA E. BARR

People's dreams are made out of what they do all day. The same way a dog that runs after rabbits will dream of rabbits. It's what you do that makes your soul, not the other way around.

BARBARA KINGSOLVER

What am I doing? Nothing. I am letting life rain upon me.

RAHEL VARNHAGEN

To do anything, it is first necessary to be doing nothing.

NANCY HALE

Idleness, simon-pure, from which all manner of good springs like seed from a fallow soil, is sure to be misnamed and misconstrued.

LOUISE IMOGEN GUINEY

Leisure and the cultivation of human capacities are inextricably interdependent.

MARGARET MEAD

On New Year's Day every calendar, large and small, has the same number of dates. But we soon learn that the years are of very different lengths.

DOROTHY CANFIELD FISHER

"Next time!" In what calendar are kept the records of those next times which never come?

HELEN HUNT JACKSON

I am sitting here in the sun
Watching the kittens playing
And the children playing
And I am convinced
There is nothing worth doing more.

SUSAN FROMBERG SCHAEFFER

To be quite oneself one must first waste a little time.

ELIZABETH BOWEN

You can kill time or kill yourself, it comes to the
same thing in the end.

ELSA TRIOLET

Stress is an ignorant state. It believes that everything
is an emergency.

NATALIE GOLDBERG

I am convinced that there are times in everybody's experience when there is so much to be done, that the only way to do it is to sit down and do nothing.

FANNY FERN

We have as much time as we need.

MELODY BEATTIE

Moments

No time like the present.

MARY DELARIVIÈRE MANLEY

Life is a continuous succession of present moments.

ELAINE ST. JAMES

The present is the point of power.

KATE GREEN

Only one person in a thousand knows the trick of really living in the present. Most of us spend fifty-nine minutes an hour living in the past, with regret for lost joys or shame for things badly done (both utterly useless and weakening) or in a future which we either long for or dread. ... There is only one minute in which you are alive, *this minute*, here and now. The only way to live is by accepting each minute as an unrepeatable minute. Which is exactly what it is—a miracle and unrepeatable.

STORM JAMESON

Happiness is a thing of now.

GLADYS TABER

My last defense
Is the present tense.

GWENDOLYN BROOKS

Just for today I will be happy. . . . Just for today I
will try to live through this day only, not to tackle
my whole life problem at once. I can do things for
twelve hours that would appall me if I had to keep
them up for a lifetime. Just for today . . .

SIBYL F. PARTRIDGE

Love the moment
and the energy
of that moment
will spread
beyond all
boundaries.

CORITA KENT

If we take care of the moments, the years will take care of themselves.

MARIA EDGEWORTH

Little drops of water,
Little grains of sand,
Make the mighty ocean
And the pleasant land.
Thus the little minutes,
Humble though they be,
Make the mighty ages
Of eternity.

JULIA A. FLETCHER

We have only this moment, sparkling like a star in our hand . . . and melting like a snowflake. Let us use it before it is too late.

MARIE EDITH BEYNON

I have no Yesterdays,
Time took them away;
Tomorrow may not be—
But I have Today.

PEARL YEADON MCGINNIS

If you let yourself be absorbed completely, if you
surrender completely to the moments as they pass,
you live more richly those moments.

ANNE MORROW LINDBERGH

Spend all you have for loveliness,
Buy it and never count the cost;
For one white singing hour of peace
Count many a year of strife well lost,
And for a breath of ecstasy
Give all you have been, or could be.

SARA TEASDALE

Every hour has its immediate duty, its special
injunction
which dominates all others.

MARGUERITE YOURCENAR

Each day provides its own gifts.

RUTH P. FREEDMAN

This moment contains
the fullness of all moments
nothing else is needed.

CORITA KENT

Life is a succession
of moments
to live each one
is to succeed.

CORITA KENT

When one cannot be sure that there are many days
left, each single day becomes as important as a year,
and one does not waste an hour in wishing that that
hour were longer, but simply fills it, like a smaller
cup, as high as it will go without spilling over.

NATALIE KUSZ

How we spend our days is, of course, how we spend
our lives.

ANNIE DILLARD

SMALL COMFORTS

One of the secrets of a happy life is continuous small treats.

IRIS MURDOCH

I am doing something I learned early to do, I am
paying attention to small beauties,
whatever I have—as if it were our duty to
find things to love, to bind ourselves to this world.

SHARON OLDS

It isn't the great big pleasures that count the most;
it's making a great deal out of the little ones.

JEAN WEBSTER

There *are* no little things. "Little things," so called, are the hinges of the universe.

FANNY FERN

The cream of enjoyment in this life is always impromptu. The chance walk; the unexpected visit; the unpremeditated journey; the unsought conversation or acquaintance.

FANNY FERN

Ah! there is nothing like staying at home, for real comfort.

JANE AUSTEN

One's own surroundings means so much to one, when one is feeling miserable.

EDITH SITWELL

Nothing makes a house cozier than cats.

GLADYS TABER

Is it enough to know that one creature likes what you do and the way you do it and that that creature is your cat?

NAOMI THORNTON

I like handling newborn animals. Fallen into life from an unmappable world, they are the ultimate immigrants, full of wonder and confusion.

DIANE ACKERMAN

When you feel really lousy, puppy therapy is indicated.

SARA PARETSKY

Dogs are the most amazing creatures; they give unconditional love. For me they are the role model for being alive.

GILDA RADNER

I know of nothing to compare with the welcome a dog gives you when you come home.

GLADYS TABER

Food is the most primitive form of comfort.

SHEILAH GRAHAM

Soup not only warms you and is easy to swallow and to digest, it also creates the illusion in the back of your mind that Mother is there.

MARLENE DIETRICH

Probably the most satisfying soup in the world for people who are hungry, as well as for those who are tired or worried or cross or in debt or in a moderate amount of pain or in love or in robust health or in any kind of business huggermuggery, is minestrone.

M.F.K. FISHER

As long ago as yesterday and as near as tomorrow, bread and soup still sustain and comfort us. Here are our primary nutrients contained in golden loaves . . . . And soup is a simmering secret of vitamins and minerals ready to nourish us and send us forth.

YVONNE YOUNG TARR

A meal, however simple, is a moment of intersection. It is at once the most basic, the most fundamental, of our life's activities, maintaining the life of our bodies; shared with others it can be an occasion of joy and communion, uniting people deeply.

ELISE BOULDING

All food starting with *p* is comfort food . . . pasta, potato chips, pretzels, peanut butter, pastrami, pizza, pastry.

SARA PARETSKY

Pistachio nuts, the red ones, cure any problem.

PAULA DANZIGER

There was something immensely comforting, I found, about a crumpet—so comforting that I've never forgotten about them and have even learned to make them myself against those times when I have no other source of supply.

PEG BRACKEN

He said I was the most sensitive person he'd ever seen—that I belonged to the hyper-hyper type and we *rarely* survive! Of course, I was examined, and so was the éclair, and they found that the éclair contains *every*thing my system lacks. So I take three a day and I feel like a new woman!

RUTH DRAPER

Chocolate is no ordinary food. It is not something you can take or leave, something you like only moderately. You don't *like* chocolate. You don't even *love* chocolate. Chocolate is something you have an *affair* with.

GENEEN ROTH

Research tells us that fourteen out of any ten individuals like chocolate.

SANDRA BOYNTON

The tea-hour is the hour of peace. . . . Strife is lost in the hissing of the kettle—a tranquilizing sound, second only to the purring of a cat.

AGNES REPPLIER

Gin is cheering and wine maketh glad the heart of man, but when you're in a real turmoil there's nothing like a good strong cup of tea.

ANTHONY GILBERT

Tea quenches tears and thirst.

JEANINE LARMOTH AND CHARLOTTE TURGEON

I stir wild honey into my carefully prepared cedar tea
and wait for meaning to arise,
to greet and comfort me.

PAULA GUNN ALLEN

Tea—that perfume that one drinks, that connecting
hyphen.

NATALIE CLIFFORD BARNEY

The urban workaday economy would be unthinkable
without coffee.

IRENE FIZER

A handwritten, personal letter has become a gen-
uine modern-day luxury, like a child's pony ride.

SHANA ALEXANDER

Always serve letters with a cup of tea and a footstool. Celebrate "the reading" slowly. It is irreverent to read a letter fast.

MACRINA WIEDERKEHR

A hot bath! How exquisite a vespertine pleasure, how luxurious, fervid and flagrant a consolation for the rigors, the austerities, the renunciations of the day.

ROSE MACAULAY

My philosophy is very simple: when in doubt, take a bath.

SARAH BAN BREATHNACH

There must be quite a few things a hot bath won't cure, but I don't know many of them.

SYLVIA PLATH

Let others, worn with living
And living's aftermath,
Take Sleep to heal the heart's distress,
Take Love to be their comfortress,
Take Song or Food or Fancy Dress,
But I shall take a Bath.

PHYLLIS MCGINLEY

I can't think of any sorrow in the world that a hot
bath wouldn't help, just a little bit.

SUSAN GLASPELL

Shunning the upstart shower,
The cold and cursory scrub,
I celebrate the power
That lies within the Tub.

PHYLLIS MCGINLEY

There is always time for a nap.

SUZY BECKER

A nap is not to be confused with sleeping. We sleep to recharge our bodies. We nap to care for our souls.

SARAH BAN BREATHNACH

The more naps you take, the more awakenings you experience.

SARAH BAN BREATHNACH

My bed is the place where it all comes together. Here is where I think naked thoughts, daydream, make love, worry, plot, argue, get my back scratched, speculate, talk about growing old, and, finally, cut the mooring ties and drift out with the dream tide. The bed, the place where we are born and die, is our primeval place.

LAURA GREEN

There is hardly any one in the civilized world—particularly of those who do just a little more every day than they really have strength to perform—who has not at some time regarded bed as a refuge.

J.E. BUCKROSE

My bed is my best friend. . . . I type in it, telephone in it, think in it, and stare at the wall from it. Some morning, a long time from now, I hope I will be found peacefully dead in it, lying in a narrow but cozy space between old manuscripts, lost books, empty teacups, misplaced nightgowns, and unsharpened pencils.

JANE O'REILLY

One cannot see callers, answer the telephone, go to luncheons or dinners, visit the dentist or shoemaker, address charitable organizations in or from a bed; therefore a bed, in my experience, is simply bristling with ideas.

KATE DOUGLAS WIGGIN

It is in bed that we learn to bear the inevitable. We are learning this all the time while we lie with our face turned to the wall thinking we are doing nothing.

J.E. Buckrose

Sleep in whenever you can. Go to bed early every night for as long as you need to. Sleep throughout the weekends. Take naps whenever possible. Relish sleep. Luxuriate in it. Grow in it. Expand in it. You need it.

Elaine St. James

If there be one hour of the twenty-four which has the life of day without its labor, and the rest of night without its slumber, it is the lovely and languid hour of twilight.

L.E. Landon

I love the night. I love to feel the tide of darkness rising, slowly and slowly washing, turning over and over, lifting, floating, all that lies strewn upon the dark beach, all that lies hid in rocky hollows.

KATHERINE MANSFIELD

Nature has been for me, for as long as I can remember, a source of solace, inspiration, adventure, and delight; a home, a teacher, a companion.

LORRAINE ANDERSON

If I had Aladdin's lamp and the usual three wishes, the first would always be, "Give me the first day of June."

GLADYS TABER

Without music I should wish to die.

EDNA ST. VINCENT MILLAY

Music, my joy, my full-scale God.

GWEN HARWOOD

If God exists
then music is his love for me.

GWEN HARWOOD

The past-that-might-have-been, and the future-that-was-to-be, stretched behind and before her, as is strangely often the case when we are listening to music.

EDNA FERBER

134

I think I should have no other mortal wants, if I could always have plenty of music. It seems to infuse strength into my limbs and ideas into my brain. Life seems to go on without effort, when I am filled with music.

GEORGE ELIOT

One of the loveliest things about being grown up is the knowledge that never again will I have to go through the miserable business of performing in Mrs. Smedley's Annual Piano Recital at McKinleyville's First Presbyterian Church.

PEG BRACKEN

Humor was for her a kind of social salt; and salt not only adds savor, it preserves.

BERTHA DAMON

When I cannot bear outer pressures any more, I
begin to put order in my belongings. . . . As if
unable to organize and control my life, I seek to
exert this on the world of objects.

ANAÏS NIN

Skiing is the next best thing to having wings.

OPRAH WINFREY

Life, after we'd had a few millennia to observe it,
turned out to be dreadfully unfair, so we invented
sports.

BARBARA HOLLAND

ET PEEVES

Don't you hate people who say they're not complaining and then complain?

EDNA FERBER

If we could make up our minds to spare our friends all details of ill health, of money losses, of domestic annoyances, of altercations, of committee work, of grievances, provocations, and anxieties, we should sin less against the world's good-humor. It may not be given us to add to the treasury of mirth; but there is considerable merit in not robbing it.

AGNES REPPLIER

Isn't it boring . . . how people always want to tell
you their own stories instead of listening to yours?
I suppose that's why psychiatrists are better than
friends; the paid listener doesn't interrupt with his
own experiences.

HELEN VAN SLYKE

When these incorrigible talkers are compelled to
be quiet, is it not evident that they are not silent
because they are listening to what is said, but
because they are thinking of what they themselves
shall say when they can seize the first lucky interval,
for which they are so narrowly watching?

HANNAH MORE

Once you get to know your neighbors, you are no
longer free, you are all tangled up, you have to stop
and speak when you are out and you never feel safe
when you are in.

ROSE MACAULAY

My dear father always said that when everybody had a telephone nobody would have any manners, because there wouldn't be time for them. And of course he was perfectly right.

PATRICIA WENTWORTH

The mail begs for everything but my life.

AGNES REPPLIER

Why does a slight tax increase cost you two hundred dollars and a substantial tax cut save you thirty cents?

PEG BRACKEN

I wish that the land-tax went a little more according to situation than it does. 'Tis really ridiculous, how one has to pay five times as much as another, without any reason that ever I heard tell.

HARRIET MARTINEAU

So-called good advice is always served with compliments and sprinkled with sugar. I don't like sugar.

VICTORIA WOLFF

The one prediction that never comes true is, "You'll thank me for telling you this."

JUDITH MARTIN

"I knew you wouldn't mind" is the formula with which my friends begin the confession that they have made use of me in some indefensible way, or written a brutal criticism of my new novel.

STORM JAMESON

All our Western thought is founded on this repulsive pretense that pain is the proper price of any good thing.

REBECCA WEST

I hate the word "ought"—it always implies something dull, cold, and commonplace. The "ought nots" of life are its pleasantest things.

L.E. LANDON

I have no faith in the sense of comforting beliefs which persuade me that all my troubles are blessings in disguise.

REBECCA WEST

People with theories of life are, perhaps, the most relentless of their kind, for no time or place is sacred from their devastating elucidations.

AGNES REPPLIER

I do dislike people with Moral Aims. Everyone asks me why I learn Arabic, and when I say I just like it, they looked shocked and incredulous.

FREYA STARK

Honesty has come to mean the privilege of insulting you to your face without expecting redress.

JUDITH MARTIN

I just wish, when neither of us has written to my husband's mother, I didn't feel so much worse about it than he does.

KATHARINE WHITEHORN

Sixty if she's a day. Calls herself forty-seven, of course. They're all forty-seven when they get past fifty.

WINIFRED HOLTBY

I have always preferred the company of older people. No one in the history of the world has had less
interest in the young than I do. I am not interested
in what young people are thinking. They're thinking
less than old people, of course. I mean, what could
they be thinking? And what are they doing? They're
doing the same stupid things you did.

FRAN LEBOWITZ

There are some people who never acknowledge
themselves in the wrong; God help them!

MARIE DE RABUTIN-CHANTAL, MARQUISE DE SÉVIGNÉ

I loathe nostalgia.

DIANA VREELAND

Progress? It ought to be stopped, that's what I say. If the Lord meant chickens to come out of incubators he'd never have made hens, it stands to reason.

WINIFRED HOLTBY

The other day I bought a wastebasket and I carried it home in a paper bag. And when I got home, I put the paper bag in the wastebasket.

JANE WAGNER AND LILY TOMLIN

Consistency is the horror of the world.

BRENDA UELAND

You may have noticed, as I have, that if ever you find yourself declaring emphatically and unequivocally that you will never do some one particular thing, chances are good that this is precisely what you will one day find yourself doing.

PEG BRACKEN

In trying to understand the appeal of best-sellers, it is well to remember that whistles can be made sounding certain notes which are clearly audible to dogs and other of the lower animals, though man is incapable of hearing them.

REBECCA WEST

Nowadays people write English as if a rat were caught in the typewriter and they were trying to hit the keys which wouldn't disturb it.

LILLIAN HELLMAN

It is imperative when flying coach that you restrain any tendency toward the vividly imaginative. For although it may momentarily appear to be the case, it is not at all likely that the cabin is entirely inhabited by crying babies smoking inexpensive domestic cigars.

FRAN LEBOWITZ

How subtle is the relationship between the traveler and his luggage! He knows, as no one else knows, its idiosyncrasies, its contents . . . and always some small nuisance which he wishes he had not brought; had known, indeed, before starting that he would regret it, but brought it all the same.

VITA SACKVILLE-WEST

I worry that the person who thought up musak may be thinking up something else.

JANE WAGNER AND LILY TOMLIN

Do you know on this one block you can buy croissants in five different places? There's one store called Bonjour Croissant. It makes me want to go to Paris and open a store called Hello Toast.

FRAN LEBOWITZ

As we understand the doctors, you can live much longer if you quit everything that makes you want to.

MARTHA LUPTON

Britt ate lots of chocolate but never got fat—a sure sign of demonic possession.

ERICA JONG

Large, naked, raw carrots are acceptable as food only to those who live in hutches eagerly awaiting Easter.

FRAN LEBOWITZ

I have just partaken of that saddest of things—a cup of *weak* tea.

KATHERINE MANSFIELD

Like many quite good medical men he regarded women as mentally deficient and physiologically malformed.

STORM JAMESON

The same people who tell us that smoking doesn't cause cancer are now telling us that advertising cigarettes doesn't cause smoking.

ELLEN GOODMAN

Now we've got smokism. It's one of the reasons I became a writer: to be able to smoke in peace.

SUSANNA KAYSEN

Many people find smoking objectionable. That is
their right. I would, I assure you, be the very last to
criticize the annoyed. I myself find many—even
most—things objectionable. Being offended is the
natural consequence of leaving one's home. I do
not like aftershave lotion, adults who rollerskate,
children who speak French, or anyone who is
unduly tan. I do not, however, go around enacting
legislation and putting up signs.

FRAN LEBOWITZ

Perhaps the greatest rudenesses of our time come
not from the callousness of strangers, but from the
solicitousness of intimates who believe that their
frank criticisms are always welcome, and who feel
free to "be themselves" with those they love, which
turns out to mean being their worst selves, while
saving their best behavior for strangers.

JUDITH MARTIN

I cannot abide the Mr. and Mrs. Noah attitude towards marriage; the animals went in two by two, forever stuck together with glue.

VITA SACKVILLE-WEST

Half the good intentions of my life have been frustrated by my unfortunate habit of putting things off till to-morrow.

MARIA EDGEWORTH

Wanton killing for sport, or euphemistically, for "management" seems to me a poor way of demonstrating our higher intelligence. Predators hunt to live. Only man hunts for the sheer triumph of killing. It is a fact that only man is uplifted by the spectacle of an animal's death.

JOAN WARD-HARRIS

Life is worth being lived, but not being discussed all the time.

ISABELLE ADJANI

The majority of critical, and plenty of uncritical, readers find quotations a bore.

ETHEL SMYTH

 HE ORDINARY

The incredible gift of the ordinary! Glory comes streaming from the table of daily life.

MACRINA WIEDERKEHR

The very commonplaces of life are components of its eternal mystery.

GERTRUDE ATHERTON

How many joys are crushed under foot because people look up at the sky and disregard what is at their feet.

CATHARINA ELISABETHA GOETHE

Greatness is to take the common things of life and walk truly among them.

RALPH IRON

Neither saints nor angels have ever increased my faith in this enigma Life; but what are called "common men and women" have increased it.

PHYLLIS BOTTOME

I am beginning to respect the apathetic days.
Perhaps they're a necessary pause: better to give in
to them than to fight them at your desk hopelessly;
then you lose both the day and your self-respect.
Treat them as physical phenomena — casually — and
obey them.

ANNE MORROW LINDBERCH

We are often like rivers: careless and forceful, timid
and dangerous, lucid and muddied, eddying, gleam-
ing, still. Lovers, farmers, and artists have one thing
in common, at least — a fear of "dry spells," dormant
periods in which we do no blooming, internal
droughts only the waters of imagination and psychic
release can civilize.

GRETEL EHRLICH

Eden is that old-fashioned House
We dwell in every day
Without suspecting our abode
Until we drive away.

EMILY DICKINSON

Oh, life — the whole of life — is far too fleet.
The things of every day are all so sweet.
The common things of life are all so dear . . .
Is Heaven not after all the Now and Here?

ALICE E. ALLEN

Normal day, let me be aware of the treasure you are.
Let me learn from you, love you, savor you, bless you
before you depart. Let me not pass you by in quest of
some rare and perfect tomorrow. Let me hold you
while I may, for it will not always be so. One day I
shall dig my nails into the earth, or bury my face in
the pillow, or stretch myself taut, or raise my hands to
the sky, and want more than all the world your return.

MARY JEAN IRION

REALITY

My greatest enemy is reality. I have fought it successfully for thirty years.

MARGARET ANDERSON

I wrestled with reality for forty years, and I am happy to state that I finally won out over it.

MARY CHASE

The most all-around, practical, long-wearing illusions are the ones that you weave yourself.

PEG BRACKEN

Reality was such a jungle—with no signposts, landmarks, or boundaries.

HELEN HAYES

Reality is a crutch for people who can't cope with drugs.

JANE WAGNER

Everything is ambiguous. It's exciting, in a way, if you can tolerate ambiguity. I can't, but I'm taking a course where it's taught, in the hope of acquiring the skill. It's called Modern Living, and you get no credit.

SHEILA BALLANTYNE

Fearful as reality is: it is less fearful than evasions of reality.

CAITLIN THOMAS

Reality can be magnificent even when life is not.

LIV ULLMANN

We live in a fantasy world, a world of illusion. The great task in life is to find reality.

IRIS MURDOCH

The people who say you are not facing reality actually mean that you are not facing *their idea* of reality.

MARGARET HALSEY

What is reality anyway? Nothin' but a collective hunch.

JANE WAGNER

Nothing, perhaps, is strange, once you have accepted life itself, the great strange business which includes all lesser strangenesses.

ROSE MACAULAY

Memory

I wear the key of memory, and can open every door in the house of my life.

AMELIA E. BARR

Some memories are realities, and are better than anything that can ever happen to one again.

WILLA CATHER

Memory, that library of the soul from which I will draw knowledge and experience for the rest of my life.

TOVE DITLEVSEN

As a life's work, I would remember everything—
everything, against loss. I would go through life like
a plankton net.

ANNIE DILLARD

How we remember, what we remember, and why
we remember form the most personal map of our
individuality.

CHRISTINA BALDWIN

In memory each of us is an artist: each of us creates.

PATRICIA HAMPL

The past is never where you think you left it.

KATHERINE ANNE PORTER

How swiftly the locks rust, the hinges grow stiff on doors that close behind us!

LADY MURASAKI

EXPERIENCE

Never regret. If it's good, it's wonderful. If it's bad, it's experience.

VICTORIA HOLT

Experience is what really happens to you in the long run; the truth that finally overtakes you.

KATHERINE ANNE PORTER

Everything you experience is what constitutes *you* as a human being, but the experience passes away and the person's left. The person is the residue.

ILKA CHASE

The fruit of life is experience, not happiness.

AMELIA E. BARR

Experience may be hard but we claim its gifts because they are real, even though our feet bleed on its stones.

M.P. FOLLETT

Experience is what you get looking for something else.

MARY PETTIBONE POOLE

Experience is a good teacher, but she sends in terrific bills.

MINNA THOMAS ANTRIM

Intuition

I am a woman
who understands
the necessity of an impulse whose goal or origin
still lie beyond me.

OLGA BROUMAS

Often intuition will direct you. If it feels right, it's probably right.

OPRAH WINFREY

One should always act from one's inner sense of rhythm.

ROSAMOND LEHMANN

We need to be willing to let our intuition guide us, and then be willing to follow that guidance directly and fearlessly.

SHAKTI GAWAIN

It is only by following your deepest instinct that you can lead a rich life and if you let your fear of consequence prevent you from following your deepest instinct, then your life will be safe, expedient and thin.

KATHARINE BUTLER HATHAWAY

I believe that we are always attracted to what we need most, an instinct leading us towards the persons who are to open new vistas in our lives and fill them with new knowledge.

HELENE ISWOLSKY

We grow in time to trust the future for our answers.

RUTH BENEDICT

Learning to trust our intuition is an art form, and like all other art forms, it takes practice to perfect.

SHAKTI GAWAIN

ELF-DETERMINATION

Of my own spirit let me be
in sole though feeble mastery.

SARA TEASDALE

Can't nothin' make your life work if you ain't the architect.

TERRY MCMILLAN

Your world is as big as you make it.

GEORGIA DOUGLAS JOHNSON

Reach high, for stars lie hidden in your soul.
Dream deep, for every dream precedes the goal.

PAMELA VAULL STARR

It is necessary to try to surpass one's self always; this
occupation ought to last as long as life.

CHRISTINA, QUEEN OF SWEDEN

Yet keep within your heart
A place apart
Where little dreams may go,
May thrive and grow.
Hold fast—hold fast your dreams!

LOUISE DRISCOLL

If you think you can, you can. And if you think you can't, you're right.

MARY KAY ASH

If you doubt you can accomplish something, then you can't accomplish it. You have to have confidence in your ability, and then be tough enough to follow through.

ROSALYNN CARTER

It is a good thing to learn early that other people's opinions do not matter, unless they happen to be true.

PHYLLIS BOTTOME

It's dangerous to start attributing your fortunes to luck and your misfortunes to fate.

NANCY PICKARD

Take your life in your own hands, and what happens? A terrible thing: no one to blame.

ERICA JONG

You can eat an elephant one bite at a time.

MARY KAY ASH

The world doesn't come to the clever folks, it comes to the stubborn, obstinate, one-idea-at-a-time people.

MARY ROBERTS RINEHART

I believe that happiness consists in having a destiny in keeping with our abilities. Our desires are things of the moment, often harmful even to ourselves; but our abilities are permanent, and their demands never cease.

MADAME DE STAËL

Any road is bound to arrive somewhere if you follow it far enough.

PATRICIA WENTWORTH

It is good to have an end to journey towards; but it is the journey that matters in the end.

URSULA K. LE GUIN

The end is nothing; the road is all.

WILLA CATHER

The journey is my home.

MURIEL RUKEYSER

I am one of those who never knows the direction of my journey until I have almost arrived.

ANNA LOUISE STRONG

Sometimes you don't know that the house you live in is glass until the stone you cast comes boomeranging back. Maybe that's the actual reason you threw it. Something in you was yelling, "I want out." The life you saved, as well as the glass you shattered, was your own.

JESSAMYN WEST

Surviving is important, but thriving is *elegant*.

MAYA ANGELOU

In my life's chain of events nothing was accidental. Everything happened according to an inner need.

HANNAH SENESH

The world is full of hopeful analogies and handsome, dubious eggs, called possibilities.

GEORGE ELIOT

Nothing is impossible, we just don't know how to do it yet.

L.L. LARISON CUDMORE

All things are possible until they are proved impossible—and even the impossible may only be so, as of now.

PEARL S. BUCK

What we seek we do not find—that would be too trim and tidy for so reckless and opulent a thing as life. It is something else we find.

SUSAN GLASPELL

When you stop looking for something, you see it right in front of you.

ELEANOR COPPOLA

Often the search proves more profitable than the goal.

E.L. KONIGSBURG

You may trod me in the very dirt
But still, like dust, I'll rise.

MAYA ANGELOU

If you don't know what you want from life, you will accept anything.

DOROTHY WINBUSH RILEY

Give to the world the best you have,
And the best will come back to you.

MADELEINE S. BRIDGES

The purpose of our lives is to give birth to the best which is within us.

MARIANNE WILLIAMSON

There is only one of you in the world, just one, and if that is not fulfilled then something has been lost.

MARTHA GRAHAM

My parents . . . always told me I could do anything but never told me how long it would take.

RITA RUDNER

Making a Difference

I am in the world
to change the world.

MURIEL RUKEYSER

One act of beneficence, one act of real usefulness,
is worth all the abstract sentiment in the world.

ANN RADCLIFFE

A life of value is not a series of great things well
done; it is a series of small things consciously done.

JOAN CHITTISTER

We can do no great things—only small things with great love.

MOTHER TERESA

My feeling is that there is nothing in life but refraining from hurting others, and comforting those that are sad.

OLIVE SCHREINER

That shall be my life, to scatter flowers—to miss no single opportunity of making some small sacrifice, here by a smiling look, there by a kindly word, always doing the tiniest things right, and doing it for love.

ST. THÉRÈSE OF LISIEUX

The richness of our own lives, creative and receptive, depends on how closely we identify ourselves with the struggles and problems, individual and social, as well as with the hopes and ideals of the age in which we live.

ANITA BLOCK

If we all tried to make other people's paths easy, our own feet would have a smooth even place to walk on.

MYRTLE REED

I firmly believe that none of us in this world have made it until the least among us have made it.

OPRAH WINFREY

The world is wide, and I will not waste my life in friction when it could be turned into momentum.

FRANCES E. WILLARD

When we do the best that we can, we never know what miracle is wrought in our life, or in the life of another.

HELEN KELLER

A vast deal may be done by those who dare to act.

JANE AUSTEN

I try. I am trying. I was trying. I will try. I shall in the meantime try. I sometimes have tried. I shall still by that time be trying.

DIANE GLANCY

The world asks of us
only the strength we have and we give it.

JANE HIRSHFIELD

We do what we can. The results are none of our business.

JENNIFER STONE

It is not our job to work miracles, but it is our task to try.

JOAN CHITTISTER

What courage and patience are wanted for every life that aims to produce anything!

GEORGE ELIOT

When you cease to make a contribution you begin to die.

ELEANOR ROOSEVELT

To be content with the world as it is is to be dead.

DOROTHEE SÖLLE

Things that don't get better, get worse.

ELLEN SUE STERN

There are always a few people you do a lot for, and a few who do a lot for you, but they're not the same people.

MIGNON MCLAUGHLIN

We are rich only through what we give, and poor only through what we refuse.

ANNE-SOPHIE SWETCHINE

To work in the world lovingly means that we are defining what we will be *for*, rather than reacting to what we are against.

CHRISTINA BALDWIN

If you don't stand for something, you will stand for anything.

GINGER ROGERS

How lovely to think that no one need wait a moment,
we can start now, start slowly changing the world!

ANNE FRANK

*T*HE QUILT OF OUR DAYS

Life's just a perpetual piecing together of broken bits.

EDITH WHARTON

Life is creation. Self and circumstances the raw
material.

DOROTHY M. RICHARDSON

Life resembles Gobelin tapestry; you do not see the
canvas on the right side; but when you turn it, the
threads are visible.

MADAME DE STAËL

It was as if I had worked for years on the wrong side of a tapestry, learning accurately all its lines and figures, yet always missing its color and sheen.

ANNA LOUISE STRONG

All is pattern, all life, but we can't always see the pattern when we're part of it.

BELVA PLAIN

As there is design and symmetry in nature, I believe there is also design and symmetry in human experience if we will learn to yield ourselves to our destinies.

KATHARINE BUTLER HATHAWAY

One should make one's life a mosaic. Let the general design be good, the colors lively, and the materials diversified.

PRINCESS MARTHE BIBESCO